Also by Toni Thomas:

Chosen
Fast as Lightening
Walking on Water
Blue Halo
Ace Raider of the Unfathomable Universe
You'll be Fast as Lightning Coveting my Painted Tail
Hotsy Totsy Ballroom
Love Adrift in the City of Stars
In the Pink Arms of the City
In the Kingdom of Longing
The Things We Don't Know
In the Boarding House for Unclaimed Girls
They Became Wing Perfect and Flew
Unburdened Kisses
Bandits Come and Remove Her Body in the Night
There is This
Here
The Smooth White Vanishing
Perishing in the Rain
A Different Measure of Moonlight
The Secret Language of River
Inside Her a River of Snow was Traveling
The Arbiter of Her Own Flame
Paradise on a Shoestring
A Bride of Amazement

A Portuguese Lullaby
is What I am After

Published 2025
Annalese Press
West Yorkshire HD9 3XZ
England

Copyright © 2023 Toni Thomas

*All characters and situations appearing in these pages are creatures of the imagination and in the service of poetry.
Any resemblance to real persons living or dead, is purely coincidental.*

All rights reserved. No part of this publication may be reproduced, stored, or transmitted in any form, or by any means electronic, mechanical or photocopying, recording or otherwise, without the express written permission of the publisher.

Cover design and layout by Peter Wadsworth
Head of the Virgin, Taddeo di Bartolo, 1397

British Library Cataloguing-in-Publication Data
A catalogue record for this book is available on request from the British Library.

ISBN 978-1-0685744-4-3

Part One *When You Come to Me*

A lullaby is what I am after	2
Sometimes the penmanship of the dark	3
If hunger has invaded me	4
How many reasons	5
Fado	6
Now that you have gone	7
My mother	8
Who says the course of love runs smooth	9
In the dry heat	10
It is not easy to make room	11
No longer the swollen mountain	12
If I sleep in the nest of you	13
Make me a room in your heart	14
Please don't make me rehearse death	15
The big dog at the inn	16
The night sleeps with me	17
In the Praca da Republica	18
In the quiet hours	19
Mother of ocean	20
When I name you	21
Tomorrow when we fetch	22
When you come to me	23

Part Two *City of Light Burning*

I taste you in the cramped corner	26
In the springtime	27
In a dry landscape	28
In Fatima	29
This city sleeps five deep	30
The man going from table to table	31
My dog will not trouble you	32
When the field is stripped	33
Perhaps the weight of repose	34
When the last dance wears out	35
When I had spent nearly all my money	36
Inside the spindle of light	37
In the language of dream	38
The day is heavy with heat	39
In the grove	40
The hours are ringing the bells	41

Part Three *Landscape of Wings*

I am the girl who lives	44
Impatient I devour your honey	45
I run around in scant clothes	46
By the bridge	47
Up on the hillsides of the Minho Valley	48
I no longer count kisses	49

Beloved, you can hear me	50
Now that the hours move	51
Love is wearing her chaste voice	52
My dress no longer stamped	53
Who would marry a misfit	54
You wear me down	55
The earth is spelling you out	56

*"My soul is a secret orchestra, but I don't know what instruments -
strings, harps, cymbals, drums - strum and bang inside me.
I only know myself as the symphony."*
                                                Fernando Pessoa

Truly to sing, that is a different breath.
                                                Heinrich Heine

Part One

When You Come to Me

A lullaby is what I am after

make it soft, fervent
make it pillow talk
a cacophony of birds
the flirty red of poppies
catastrophe gone for a ride
with the faith of rivers.

A lullaby is what I am after.
Let it resemble my mother's lips
the purple parrot alive on a stick

let it come out of nowhere
the trickster wind
commotion of rain

let it seize me
toss my hair, my skirt, my words
till they fly.

Sometimes the penmanship of the dark

takes things hostage
will choke on your food
then ask for more

as if life is a pebbled road
thorny enterprise
brushed with rivals.

But then some things
get halted mid-sentence
become a hacked room
tangle of kisses.

What would it be like
to enter a soulful death
with a choir of children singing?

If hunger has invaded me

with its prickly voice
broken chairs
charred remains of a house

then who will blame me
for setting a light to what
remains of this table
entering your season
to claim it as my own.

If something has eluded me
stolen my will
if my kisses get snatched
by a coal black sky

will you care
still come running
as if I mean something?

How many reasons

to be here
admit death as it flies
round out the rough edge of seasons
torn limbs
money with its paper sails
hunger?

Sometimes you speak
a strange tongue
I am lost in a landscape
that refuses to marry me.
Bread is scarce.
No one listens.

Sometimes I can't see the stars
bed in Porto, Lisbon, Setubal
scrape the plate of my sleep
anxious to find you.

Fado

In the strings of the fevered guitar
city's lost minstrels
woman fanning her stones of sorrow
I hear your voice

not combed perfect
sonorous as the bees mating
but insistent
reaching for an armload of stars
bread to live by.

In the roses dying on my brow
I hear your voice
climb through the centuries
made of mud and hurt
loam and wind
the scent of the forest.

In the peeled down raw
of this night season
I hear you call to me
call to me
plaintive.

Now that you have gone

I am only half a pencil
half a face, half a body.
All night the territory of dread
travels me.

Now that you have gone
the woman polishing stars
has vanished
roses slump
my words are not my own
not my own.

Now that you have gone
my kisses speak parched
stone upon stone bleeding

everything I have ever loved
a broken vow
shaved continent.

My mother

is combing my sister's hair
in hope she will find a decent job
husband
goes to mass, prays on her knees
as if God protects the loyal, the fallen
sees into our heart's furnace
props up a rustproof meadow.

I try to tell her *the day is three parts dirt*
a sea of longing
but she does not listen.

My mother travels by boat
can knock against shoals, loss
stay the tide's loyal friend
an unschooled ocean.

Some of us are gnarled roots
hapless birds
a symphony of nails
want to rise up above the savage
drink the forest
puncture the sky's listless longing
with our lips.

Who says the course of love runs smooth

the fruit of the tree will always survive
a drought of stones.

Some houses shut their windows
dine on slant light
fiction
others turn the stranger into poem.

Not all things proceed unbroken.
Not all words are harmless.
In the dark tower of love
bodies can turn foreign
vows take on an odd life
all their own.

In the dry heat

when the hills of Porto are a crowd
of shuttered windows
dust coated laundry
when my dress sticks to my thighs
the dog pants thirst into the noonday air

when the steps are many
the hours long
the shade scarce

will I look for mercy
in the body's blue flame
as if beneath this tangle of streets
the good river of your blood
remains a fountain?

It is not easy to make room

find the silent meadow
not easy to invite some different
measure of sweetness

mount the stair wreckless
uncertain of how we'll come back.

No longer the swollen mountain

let me kneel
where the night bugs pulse
the trees whisper *holy*
let me enter the measure
of your room
eat from this other plate.

Soon enough darkness will come
rob my intentions
soon enough my children
will travel their elsewheres
my lover will lick the chamber of death

soon enough my house will vanish
and I will be left shoeless
empty again
virginal
knocking.

If I sleep in the nest of you

light a flame
offer up companionable bread
sooth words

will my life turn different
take on the scent of lemon
cinnamon, abelia

will the bindweed speak
birds fly out of the sky's purse
jubilant as a feast day

the sea teach me
her secret language of tides?

Make me a room in your heart

fragrant with pine cone, cedar
cake and feathers
lavender splashed on a spring dress

make me a room
round as your belly
a petal worth prizing
feast of birds
rain tapping rhythm and thunder.

In a dry region
half ruined landscape
make me the palpable bride
flutter of chimes
bread for the hungry
one who kisses the day
awake each dawn
grateful.

Please don't make me rehearse death

sing its notes single file
like a church processional
my first communion spelt backwards.

Sometimes hope can feel
like a two headed coin
hard to swallow

a fabricated wish
stolen vow
cemetery stricken with briars.

The big dog at the inn

with a lush view of the Serra Da Lousa
cannot ask for mercy
just barks, rattles his chain
morning, afternoon, night
as if the world is foreign
people stay stranger.

The dog on the chain
may not know a shade tree
the language of kisses
how to curl on a couch
be combed gentle.

If this dog could speak
beyond the rattle of his chain
insistence of his bark
what would he say to us
tell me – what would he say?

The night sleeps with me

a sad hotel
broken chalice.

Outside on the patio
the perfume of magnolia
dogs barking
last night's dinner crumbs
being carried away by ants.

To be alone with my thoughts
is to feel the flash of your lips
pulse of your face
snow.

The night sleeps with me.
Can it cure my aching back
the world's greed
cast your wind into
my body's prism

come to me
generous
free?

In the Praca da Republica

please bring me a lullaby
something made of egg yolk, pastry
the ribbon of poems

bring me faithful hands
to nurse the barley
feather the ears of a child.

In the Praca da Republica
make believe you love me
my stumbling blocks are no hedge
that even in the midst of winter
the moon will refuse to turn cold.

In the quiet hours

when the heat is a twilight away
my aunt Ida walks her dog
two fields over
a mile from the highway.

Who is to tell her the world is broken
when her faith says otherwise
who will help mend the fence
feed her goats
be the lover never deluded by money

the one who comes to her
not as a silver salver
but ripe with the scent of rosemary
simplicity of daisies?

Mother of ocean

still the tides of my soul
till I can ride your waves steady
even under a bat black sky
punctuated with thunder.

Mariner of ships
tether my sail, ambitions
till they stay rhymed
to your seasons of sunrise.

Mother of ocean
moist epistle
friend to the bruised
the hungry
the strange, forgotten

glint of the sun
you spoon my waters
silver.

When I name you

as irreplaceable
the one who has stolen my heart
maybe nobody will be listening.

It will be a humid day
the wet from last night's rain
gleaming the trees
stenciled across the pavement.

When I name you
as my one and only
will everything I have ever loved
come back
the clouds drift lazy
the sun break through
scented with cedar?

Tomorrow when we catch

the train to Braga
and my mind is filled with
the steep slope of your river
pine trees
love lost and love found

tomorrow when we board that train
do not ask me to extol virtue
pin only *victory* to my childhood
become beauty bright with a plastic flame.

When I board the train to Braga
please accept the scars up my arm
world's uneasy devotion
how I tried to clutch you tight
but became lost.

When you come to me

with your pale hands
uncomplicated by the world's reason

come to me open
a welcoming well
the day in love with its own body

when you come to me
broken up yet whole
my life a turntable of
washcloths and work

when you come to me
your heart sticky
your faith a firmament I can hold

please do not call me *stranger*
the one who mines things
takes what is yours, spends

don't see me as just a wish list
hapless girl bailing water
make me your own.

Part Two

City of Light Burning

I taste you in the cramped corner

of my lover's face
half gilded mirror
washerwoman's weary
taste you in the goat cheese from Minh
the maize, seeded bread
olives and potato.

Sometimes your face is more mine
than the one I carry
we travel through fado bars
gypsy linen
the street's restless.

Sometimes you slip into my sleep sac
become twin
our bodies a city of light
burning.

In the springtime

when you call my name
tell me the wind has ears
the tongue of the dark
dines on river

in the springtime
when you call my name
call the hawk, sedge, rockrose
tell me no one's hand
no one's heart
will be left empty

in the springtime
when you call my name
let me be ready
silent
willing.

In a dry landscape

people must turn the dust
of the field into friend.
The girl in the cotton shift
slips into sandals
searches shade
a wordless road
into the heat of love.

In a dry landscape
things smell of cracked earth
slumped roses
dust and traffic.
Beyond
a hidden beach
ancient tides.

To kiss your hand
the girl reaches back
and back
into tooled lace
her mother's stories
the slow
very slow steps of Jesus.

In Fatima

the miracle seeded
a young girl
amid wind and dust
eucalyptus
whispers of children.

In Fatima
the future hums
with the thirst of bees
fields' grateful
visitation and rites.
To fall down on our knees
is no measure of weakness.

In Fatima
the bugs speak holy
the grass listens
things rise up
rise up

call it love
call it fruition.

This city sleeps five deep

and then some
amid heavy clotheslines
louvered windows
the snake of alleys.

This city sleeps with want
plates of swordfish
bottles of port
street musicians, coin
love gone cheap for the asking

sleeps beside the cathedral
where streets rust
stray dogs wander.

The woman in the thin dress waits.
Birds rise bench to roof to tree.
The sky watches.

The man going from table to table

has hollow cheeks
a thin body, begging cup
speaks in Portuguese
words I don't understand
is looking for something
that sutures loss
keeps the stomach
from empty.

And I want to say
I am the faithful servant
will interrupt my meal
to search for a coin
but this is not true

yet all afternoon
the face of this man follows me
his bone thin fingers
bird pecked voice

and I wonder
where has he gone to
where will he sleep.

My dog will not trouble you

for what is not hers
does not live by hunger
fancy new things
hold a grudge for what
she might have deserved
that's gone missing

prefers grass
the thick rub of trees
sewer grates and lampposts
newly found bones.

My dog will not trouble you
for what is not hers
sniffs and licks
offers up kisses
lets you know
by the wag of her tail
body's shimmy
everyone is welcome here
special.

When the field is stripped

of its sheep
season of infants

when the day no longer recognizes
the night's twin slipper

may I be the one
who refuses to pronounce
the world as only *crippled*

let me mount the staircase
to your heart
empty
willing
naked.

Perhaps the weight of repose

cannot harm me now
and the sea has worn smooth
the shape of my heart

perhaps my old sorrows
have fled
I need no more new sunsets
to memorize your love.

Perhaps every morsel
of bread is precious
the consolation of strangers
is a meal

I need to climb
no more mountains
fan the flames of discontent
till they scorch.

Perhaps now I can sweep house
wander back into your forest
vouchsafe the animals
step down from this torn branch
whole.

When the last dance wears out

and my earthly lover has vanished
when I pine for you
like a guest missing her bed chamber

then who would I be to deny
the crooked terms of love at my door
the way you inch up the stairs flawless
offer me the flame of your wick

who would I be to argue about the terms
the timing
how your kisses win out
scatter the earth's bluebells

all my former lives
former loves
come home to nest.

When I had spent nearly all my money

given my children a decent home
watched them grow and leave
when my years shrank and death
no longer seemed like a far-fetched word
then I began to relearn music
note by note
chord by chord

as if my fingers hold wind
flight, trees, grass
loss
a porous landscape

nothing needs to remain
pinched down forever.

Inside the spindle of light

the moon offers up
I begin to fashion my new dress
twine of beeswax and pearl
seaweed and pine scent.

It is slow work.
Sometimes the nights are thin
plates at the table sit empty.

But I refuse to be the handmaid
who deserts things
fondles the tree
then forgets.

In the still hour
when the crowded world is too much
I rearrange tiny rooms
for you
trumpet my wettest kiss.

In the language of dream

that is half way between sleep
and knowing
I fasten my shoes
fasten my heart's beehive.

Wind ruffles the plain
houses nest in the sky's meadow
old people tuck sugar
into the moon's kerchief.

In the language of dream
fish fly
the night is a starry constellation
of wolves
tables yank themselves loose
make off with the lonely jazz singer.

The day is heavy with heat

bugs, stray cats
people looking for a glint of shade
the memory of blossoms.
The Republica crowded with shops
outdoor cafes patient to tempt us
under the lip of their awning.

Amid plates of sardine, stew, potato
the narrow snake of cobbled alleys
I think of you
your willingness to pronounce
the world decent.

Later the waiter will rise up on tiptoe
watch your hands map
my body's white trellis
with the speech of birds.

In the grove

when the hours still
when buds refuse to dwarf on the tree
when sunset arrives half a promise
a tease of lace

in the grove
where his kisses were always
a tangle of goodbye, misgivings
where my shadow lengthened
beneath the palm tree
do not think I have eaten the shrew bread
will be cursed forever.

In the grove
where hours still
oranges hang plump with juice
in this place I lost my first kiss
but found the will to my voice

see how I climb the rungs of sorrow
drink from your invisible well
approach night with the stubborn
stab of my singing.

The hours are ringing the bells

of your cathedral
ringing my heart dry
of thin worship
cobwebs.

See how I fall out of my house
my dress
my past

see how the trees befriend
the sky relearns my voice
unbroken

see how my certitudes
tumble
my first shoes come back
nameless now
dancing.

Part Three

Landscape of Wings

I am the girl who lives

on a limb
half broken prophecy
caught between loss and fancy.

You can see me
when the sun no longer tangles
twilight slips into her unbruised dress.

And as for the man in the blue suit
the one who walks into exits
carries the pale gauze of winter

how can he resist
this nectar that petals me
the way stars rock tumble
to a shine in my mouth

how can he deny
my moment in the sun
the luxurious of your honey?

Impatient I devour your honey

lick the sides of the jar
let my kisses spill out
spooned nectar

impatient I hoist up my skirt
shout your name in the
rooms of my trespass
clear table, set plate
bake cake for the wide
of your mouth's orchard

impatient I lick the trees
marigold, vetch
whittle want
pebble my voice
with your grapes.

I run around in scant clothes

witness the god of good things
scatter seed, bread crumb
invite deer, fox, goat
sedge, marigold
into our meadow.

Cicada twitch
their tymbals to sing.
The roofs of the tiny
houses answer.

By the bridge

Minerva is dancing
doesn't mind the uneven cobbles
way foreigners rush past
doesn't mind the hour is late
there is no potato for the supper.

By the bridge
Minerva is dancing
pigeons peck
gulls spread wing
the Douro River answers.

Up on the hillsides of the Minho Valley

farmers treat their goats
as honored guest
offer up winged voice
thick grass, music
a loyal sunset

groom with feather brush
the hand's thick honey
as if all beings are meant
to know tender.

To eat this cheese
is to taste Vivaldi, Chopin
folk ballads
feast.

I no longer count kisses

wager a bet for my meals
train the dog to bark
the night to memorize
the sky's stolen sheep

no longer angle my love
on the scales of worship
make you dance as my groom
to a perfect pitch.

Nights will come
when every kiss, stranger
what I have dreamt, lost
even my tissue thin excuses
turn friend.

Beloved, you can hear me

stumbling amid rooms
the disarray of curtains
my children's nap time

hear me between pots and pans
frying the garlic, the eggs
between straightening sheets
laundering the shirts
of the man I love.

Beloved, you can see me among stones
filling the dog's bowl, finch feeder
hosing the beans, onion, tomato
see me riding up and down
the hills of my longing

can watch me idle
when the hour allows
taste the scent of your pine
salt of your sea air
remember.

Now that the hours move

in and out without logic
my countless versions of love
are put to rest in your curative bed

now that the sorrows that once
invaded me
can no longer harm

let me be the one
who comes to you
loaded with poppies

gifts you with the heft
the best of me
comes open
unhindered
soft.

Love is wearing her chaste voice

casual sandals, halter dress
won't stab the dark
stand on a podium, demand rights.

Love is wearing her mother of pearl
Douro River, valley of vineyards
licking the clouds, cobbled streets
not making a fuss with the waiter.

Love is rinsing off soot
soothing the goats
greening the meadow
offering up fish stew
sunset.

Love is slipping into my skirt
not as the wise leading the wise
but broken down, simple
a diet you can live on
landscape of wings.

My dress no longer stamped

in the sad hotel
you once etched in me
I go around shoeless
invite the birds
secret rosebuds.

Mother of sky
mother of oceans
you ripen the field
offer up bread, olives, tomato
many poems
offer up the bee's nectar

for the thirsty man - stars in his pocket
for the dog - a bone
for the child - a bridge to travel on
for the old woman – a bench

in my ear – music.

Who would marry a misfit

like me
unfold their sleeping mat
in this unholy town
hope for kisses that turn out
to be half borrowed
a seamstress of split ends?

But somehow when the wind sings
you wager no penalty
forgive me
set the sky on fire

call to me, call to me
as your one and only.

You wear me down

with your faith's elocution
candles burning bright
beneath icons of Mary
wear me down
with your lack of pretense
easy stroll amid the pigeons.

When supper comes
no meal will be too basic
to absent the width of your praise
the lettuce sings
tomatoes jewel the salad
sardines nest like a monk.

Where would I go without the
unschooled of your meadow
voice's forgiveness?

You are the cup, the fountain
the forlorn, the saved.
Mythic deer roam your forest
stars muddy their skirt in your voice.

Look how you come to me
open, porous
lick up the rain
invite me to sip nectar
from a petaled cup.

The earth is spelling you out

in quiet prayer
the elocution of river
spelling you out in greens and tomato
the hemisphere of the ocean
raised sails

the earth is spelling you in bright kisses
fair thee wells, the hint of return
shells and seaweed

the earth is polishing your eyes
pestering you with sheep, goats
making your heart weep
rejoice
causing the boy to sing
cows to amble

the earth is spelling you as good bread
the road less taken
the summer bride who refuses
to let her soul rust.

No need to woe us with more
this twilight fielded in sweet peas
bindweed, rockrose
is enough.

Toni Thomas lives in Portland, Oregon. Her poems have been published in Austria, Spain, New Zealand, Canada, England, Scotland, and Australia. In the United States her work has appeared in over fifty literary magazines including *Prairie Schooner, North Dakota Quarterly, Hayden's Ferry Review, the Minnesota Review, Notre Dame Review, Poetry East*, and more. She has been twice nominated for a Pushcart prize, and won several awards. She has published twenty-five collections of poetry and six books for children.

Her figurative clay sculptures have been shown in gallery exhibits in Portland and Chicago, displayed in literary magazines, and housed in private collections in the U.S. and England.

Her short documentary *One of Us* was shown at the Trans-ideology: Nostalgia festival in Berlin and at the Museum of Contemporary Art in Taipei.

Since Toni loves to create and sits buried in reams of poems, manuscripts, clay figures and images….she likes to imagine all of them out in the world swaying wild as the lupine.

tonithomaspoetry.com

www.ingramcontent.com/pod-product-compliance
Lightning Source LLC
Chambersburg PA
CBHW030457010526
44118CB00011B/986